Merry Christmas to Benning
from
Uncle Frank Benning
1981.

# OVER BUTTONWOOD BRIDGE

By V. Gilbert Beers

Illustrated by Helen Endres

MOODY PRESS • CHICAGO

# What You Will Find in This Book

## CHILDREN OF COURAGE

## TOWARD A NEW LAND

## WOMEN WHO DARED

## THE WEEK WE REMEMBER

## MINI'S WORD LIST

© 1978 by V. Gilbert Beers
**Library of Congress Cataloging in Publication Data**
Beers, Victor Gilbert, 1928-
  Over Buttonwood Bridge.

  (The Muffin family picture Bible)
  SUMMARY: A collection of selected Bible stories accompanied by corresponding contemporary stories involving the imaginary Muffin family.
  1. Bible stories, English. [1. Bible stories. 2. Christian life—Fiction]
I. Endres, Helen. II. Title.
BS551.2.B439   220.9'505   78-13103
ISBN 0-8024-6266-9

*Printed in the United States of America*

## TO PARENTS AND TEACHERS

Too often truth is presented to your children without joy. And too often joy is presented to them without truth. Many parents search for a place where the two meet. Perhaps you were one of those fortunate children who found such a place of delight.

One such meeting place is Buttonwood Bridge. Gather here with your children, and learn with delight life's greatest truths from the Scriptures. Join the Muffin Family as its fun-filled adventures present serious biblical truths to your children.

This is the fourth book in The Muffin Family Picture Bible series. *Through Golden Windows*, *Under the Tagalong Tree*, and *With Sails to the Wind* have already introduced your children to the adventures of the Muffin Family.

You will recognize that the Bible stories in this book are a retelling of the Scriptures, so you may wish to use the Bible itself as you read the adventures of the Bible and the Muffin Family to your children.

# CHILDREN OF COURAGE

# Who Was That Calling?

**1 SAMUEL 3**

Samuel watched the lamps on the great lampstand flicker as he lay down on his bed. He yawned, then turned his head so he could watch the lamps until he fell asleep.

As the boy Samuel lay in this special room of the tabernacle, he thought of the things that had happened that day. In the morning, he had helped the old priest, Eli, clean the lampstand.

That afternoon, as people came to sacrifice animals at the altar, he had been shocked to see how Eli's sons, Hophni and Phinehas, had taken much more of the meat than the Lord had said they should have.

*How can the Lord bless their work?* Samuel wondered, almost aloud. *They are always doing things that the Lord has said they should not do. How can the Lord let them do Eli's work when he is gone? And if they can't do it, who will?*

6

With all of these thoughts racing through his mind, young Samuel fell fast asleep. Then he heard a voice calling to him.

"Samuel! Samuel!" the voice called.

Samuel sat up in bed. He was wide awake now.

*Who called?* Samuel wondered. *It must have been Eli. Perhaps he needs something.*

Samuel ran to the place where Eli lay sleeping. "What do you want?" Samuel asked. "You called for me?"

Eli looked sleepily at Samuel. "No, I didn't call for you," he said. "Go back to bed."

Samuel went back to bed, but he could not go back to sleep. If Eli did not call, who did?

Suddenly Samuel heard the voice call to him again. "Samuel! Samuel!" the voice said.

Samuel ran to Eli's bedside again. "You called for me again," said Samuel. "What can I do for you?"

Eli sat up in bed and looked sleepily at Samuel again. "No, I did not call for you," he said. "Go to sleep!"

Samuel lay down on his bed again and wondered about the voice. *I'm sure I heard someone calling me,* Samuel thought. *It must have been Eli. Perhaps he was calling in his sleep.*

Then Samuel heard the voice call to him a third time. Once more he ran to Eli. "I heard your voice calling again," said Samuel. "What can I do for you?"

Old Eli did not look sleepily at Samuel this time. He had been thinking about the voice. Now he knew who was calling.

"God is calling you," said Eli. "If He speaks to you again, tell Him you will listen to what He says."

Samuel lay quietly on his bed now, watching the flickering lights on the lampstand and wondering if God would call his name again. He wondered also why God would call his name instead of Eli's. He was just a boy, and Eli was the priest of all Israel.

"Samuel! Samuel!" the voice called again.

"I am listening," Samuel answered. "Tell me what You want to say, Lord."

"I will punish Eli and his sons," God said. "Hophni and Phinehas cannot be priests when Eli dies."

When morning came, Eli asked Samuel what God had said to him. But Samuel was afraid to tell him.

"You must tell me everything," Eli said.

Then Samuel told Eli what God had said to him. Eli was very quiet when he heard those things.

"God must do what He knows is best," Eli said softly. He knew then that Samuel would become the priest of Israel instead of his own sons.

Thus God arranged for Samuel to be His priest over Israel. He spoke to Samuel at other times, for Samuel tried to please Him. As the years passed, Samuel became a great man of God, serving Him as well as he could.

WHAT DO YOU THINK?

*What this story teaches:* God has great plans for those who love Him, even when they are children.

1. What makes you think that Samuel pleased God more than Eli's sons did?

2. What did God say to Samuel? How do you think Samuel felt about this? How do you think Eli felt about it?

# Over Buttonwood Bridge

"It's not fair!" Maxi grumbled. "BoBo got an A in social studies and I got a B."

"So what's wrong with that?" Mini asked.

"BoBo cheated every time he could, and I didn't," said Maxi. "That's what's wrong. Why does God let people get by with things like that?"

Poppi Muffin put down his newspaper. "How about a story?" he asked. "Perhaps we can answer your question that way."

Maxi and Mini were always ready for a story. Even Ruff and Tuff joined in the fun. This is the story Poppi told:

There was once a great king who lived on the other side of Buttonwood Bridge. His land was a wonderful land, and his castle was more beautiful than any you have ever seen.

The greatest honor in all the land was to be a knight for the king, for his knights took his messages to people everywhere. But not everyone could be a knight; only those who were faithful and true to the king got to be knights.

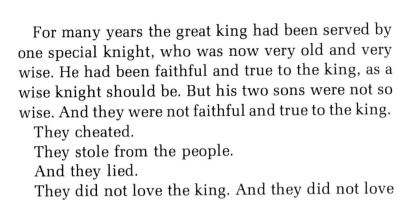

For many years the great king had been served by one special knight, who was now very old and very wise. He had been faithful and true to the king, as a wise knight should be. But his two sons were not so wise. And they were not faithful and true to the king.

They cheated.

They stole from the people.

And they lied.

They did not love the king. And they did not love the king's people.

"Why should we try to please the king?" the sons would say. "He doesn't know what is happening. And he will make us special knights because of our father. After all, who else would become his knights? There is no one else here but this servant boy."

The servant boy saw how the knight's sons lied, stole, and cheated the people. This made him very sad. He wanted to be faithful and true to the great king.

*How can the great king let them get by with such things?* he often wondered. *How can he let them become his special knights?*

One night the servant boy began to think of these things as he lay down to sleep. He watched the candle in his room flicker and wondered if the great king did know about the sons and their ways.

"But who else can the great king choose to be his special knights?" he said aloud.

"I will choose you!" a voice answered.

The servant boy sat up quickly and looked around the room. Suddenly he saw the great king himself, standing beside the door. The servant boy ran and knelt before the great king.

The great king put his hand gently but firmly on the servant boy's shoulder. "When the right time comes, you will be the most honored knight in all the land," the great king said. "But the old knight's sons cannot be so honored, for they have not been faithful and true to me."

How surprised the old knight and his sons were when they heard what had happened. But what could they say? The great king had spoken!

Maxi and Mini were very quiet for a while. "That sounds like the story of Samuel in the tabernacle that we read last night," said Mini.

"Could be," Poppi answered. "Perhaps both stories tell the same thing. Perhaps they both remind you that God may let some things happen for a while, but He makes His best plans for those who are faithful and true to Him."

LET'S TALK ABOUT THIS

*What this story teaches:* We may get by with some things for a while, but God's best plans are for those who are faithful and true to Him.

1. How does this story remind you of the story of the boy Samuel?
2. What did the great king expect from a knight? What does God expect from those of us who serve Him?
3. In what ways can you be faithful and true to God?

# The Boy King
## 2 KINGS 11

"Kill all of those children," wicked Queen Athaliah shouted.

"Those children" were her own grandchildren. She wanted to kill them so that she could rule the land. Her son, King Ahaziah, was dead. If she could kill all of his children, she could become ruler instead of one of them.

But before anyone noticed, one little baby was taken away by his Aunt Jehosheba, who lived with her husband, the priest Jehoiada, in the Temple.

Jehosheba hid the baby Joash with his nurse in a storeroom in the Temple and warned them to be quiet. For some strange reason, Joash was not missed when all the other children were killed.

During the next six years, Joash and his nurse lived quietly in the storeroom of the Temple while wicked Queen Athaliah ruled the land.

"When can we proclaim him king?" Jehosheba often asked.

"We will wait until he is seven," Jehoiada would answer. "We must be patient."

At last the time came for Joash to be proclaimed king. Jehoiada secretly called for all of the royal guards to come to the Temple.

"I have a secret, but you must promise to keep it your secret, too," he said.

"We promise," the royal guards answered.

When Jehoiada showed them the boy king, the guards were very happy, for they did not want wicked Queen Athaliah to rule the land. Then they listened to Jehoiada's plan.

"On the Sabbath day, a third of you will guard the palace, where the new king will live," Jehoiada said. "The rest of you will come here to the Temple and guard the king. Stay with him at all times, and kill anyone who tries to hurt him."

The plan worked exactly as they had hoped. At the right time, a third of the guards went to the palace, and the rest went to the Temple. Jehoiada armed the guards with the weapons he had hidden in the Temple.

Jehoiada then called to the people who had come to the Temple to worship. While they watched, he brought out Joash and placed a crown upon his head.

"Long live King Joash!" shouted Jehoiada.

"Long live the king!" shouted the people.

Everyone made so much noise that wicked Queen Athaliah rushed over to the Temple to see what was happening. Imagine her surprise when she saw Joash wearing the crown and heard the people shouting, "Long live the king!" There were trumpets blowing and sounds of happiness everywhere.

14

"Treason! Treason!" the queen shouted. "I rule this land! Not Joash!"

Athaliah was so angry that she began to tear her clothes. She could not think of letting a little boy become the ruler instead of her.

But the queen did not realize that God was helping that little boy become king. And God's helpers, the priest and his wife, were the faithful people who had made it happen.

"Take that wicked woman away and kill her," Jehoiada shouted to the guards.

The guards seized the wicked queen and took her to the palace stables, where they killed her. Then Jehoiada called for the people to give themselves to God and ask Him to be their God. He also called for the new king to rule his people well and for the people to serve their new king well.

The people realized now that they should serve God and help Him rule through the new king. So they quickly tore down the idols they had worshiped. Then they took Joash to the palace, and he became the ruler of all the land. The people were happy now, for they knew that their new ruler would help them live for God. They were free from the wicked queen at last.

WHAT DO YOU THINK?

*What this story teaches:* God helps to make, or to take away, the rulers of a nation.

1. Why did the wicked queen want to kill her own grandchildren? Why didn't she kill the boy Joash?

2. How did God help Joash become the next king? How did God's priest, Jehoiada, help to make this happen? What makes us think that the people were happy with the way this happened? Why is it important to know that God rules over all kings and kingdoms?

# The King

"Why all the excitement?" Mommi Muffin asked. "I've never seen you in such a hurry to get to school."

Maxi brushed the last hair in place and ran for the front door. "We're having tryouts this morning for our school play, 'The King,' and I'm going to get the part of the king," said Maxi.

"You're *going* to get it?" asked Mommi. "I thought these were tryouts."

"They are!" Maxi answered as he ran down the walk. "But I'm still going to get this part. It's the best one. All the other boys' parts are just servants and stuff."

When he got to school, Maxi was still sure that he would get the part of the king. But when he walked into the room where the tryouts were to be held, he gulped. There were Pookie, Tony, BoBo, and Big Bill Bluffalo.

"You—you guys trying out for servants?" he asked weakly.

"*Servants?*" they all said together. "We're trying out for the king!"

Maxi gulped twice now. He wasn't so sure that he would get the part with all those fellows trying out.

"Do you know all the lines?" Maxi asked.

"I do," said Pookie. "I've skipped TV all week to memorize them."

"Me, too," said the others.

Maxi had a strange, sinking feeling now. They all seemed so sure that they knew the lines.

"But—but we can't all be the king," said Maxi. "Teacher says whoever doesn't become king has to be a servant."

Big Bill began to chuckle. "Sorry about that, kid," he said with a laugh. "You don't mind being a servant, do you?"

Maxi knew his face was red, but he didn't answer. Of course he would mind being Big Bill's servant.

Before long the teacher stood up before the group. "We'll start with the parts for the woodcutter's wife and the princess first," said the teacher. "The king is last. Those boys who don't make the king's part will be the servants. All right?"

"Yek," all of the boys whispered under their breath.

"Oh, yes," the teacher added. "Just one other thing. I want to remind you that I'm the director of the play. It's my job to choose the king. You may not like my choice at first, but you must learn to like it, for that's the way the king must be chosen."

Maxi and his friends were not too concerned about the parts for the woodcutter's wife, the princess, or the other parts for the girls. They were all thinking about the part each wanted the most—the king.

"He gets to wear a beautiful robe!" Pookie whispered.

"And a crown," added BoBo.

"And he orders the servants to do things," Big Bill said with a chuckle.

18

At last it was time for tryouts for the king's part. Big Bill was first.

Bill was so sure he would win that he walked up onto the stage as though he owned the school. Bill threw out his chest and said his lines. Then he turned and bowed as he walked down the steps. But suddenly Bill missed a step and tumbled down to the floor, knocking the poor teacher into the other boys. Within two seconds the teacher and the boys were picking themselves up from the floor.

"Ham!" grumbled BoBo.

By the time Pookie reached the stage, he was so nervous that he forgot some important lines. BoBo got stage fright and sounded more like a recording than a real king. Maxi was so nervous by this time that he "messed up" some of his lines, as he told his friends later. Tony was the only one who did a good job.

"Looks like Tony is the king," said the teacher.

"And we're the servants," croaked Big Bill. "Yek. Who wants to be a servant?"

"We do!" said Maxi. "Tony did the best job, and we know it. So when teacher says he's king, then we're going to be good servants."

"I'd still rather be a king," said Bill, BoBo, and Pookie together.

"Me, too!" said Maxi. "But we can't. So let's be happy doing what we can do."

LET'S TALK ABOUT THIS

*What this story teaches:* We must learn to accept the leaders who are chosen for us and the things God gives us to do.

1. In what way was the teacher's choice of "the king" like God's choice of real kings? How does this remind you of God's choice of King Joash?
2. What did Maxi say about being happy as servants? Are you happy when you don't get first place in things? Can you be? Why?
3. Look up Mark 10:42-45. What did Jesus say there about becoming a king? How can you serve Jesus?

# Impossible!
### ACTS 12:1-17

"Lord, help Peter escape from prison!"

Peter's friends were praying together at the house of Mary, John Mark's mother. They were pleading with God to do something impossible—to help Peter get out of Herod's prison.

It was Passover time, and Herod had wanted to do something special for the Pharisees and their friends. What would be more special than to have their enemy, Peter, thrown into prison and then put to death?

These men hated Peter because he had told many that Jesus was alive. Hadn't they put Jesus to death themselves?

"Guard this man or die!" Herod had warned his prison guards.

"It is impossible for him to escape," said the guards. They put Peter in chains and bound him. They locked the doors. Then they placed sixteen guards around him to be sure that he would not escape.

But still the people at Mary's house prayed.

20

Peter was sure that he would die the next day. How could he ever escape from his chains, sixteen guards, and a locked iron door? There was no way. It was impossible!

But that night while his friends kept on praying, Peter fell asleep. His guards fell asleep, too.

Suddenly Peter felt something or someone hit him on the side. He looked around. Standing by his side was an angel.

"Get up and get dressed," the angel said.

Peter quickly obeyed. As he did, his chains fell to the ground.

"Follow me," the angel said.

The angel walked past the sleeping guards, with Peter behind him. But there was the great iron prison door. It was impossible to get through it.

The angel just touched the door, however, and it swung open. Then the angel and Peter walked into the quiet street of the city. Suddenly Peter was alone. The angel was gone.

Peter hurried through the dark streets toward the house where his friends were praying. When he reached the courtyard of the house, he knocked softly at the gate.

Peter's friends could not hear him knocking, for they were all praying inside the house. But a little girl named Rhoda was playing near the gate. She heard the knocking and looked outside. She could hardly believe her eyes or her ears when she heard Peter's voice.

"Peter!" she whispered.

"Let me in!" said Peter.

But Rhoda was so excited that she ran into the house shouting, "Peter! Peter! He's at the gate!"

"Sh!" said someone. "We're praying for Peter to get out of prison!"

"But he's outside at the gate!" Rhoda said. "Let him in."

The friends just sat there and shook their heads. "No, it is impossible," they said. "Peter is in prison with chains on him and guards around him. We must pray for him."

But Rhoda kept on telling the people that Peter wasn't in prison. He was outside, waiting to come in.

"I know," said someone. "It's his angel. They have killed him."

"Sh!" said another. "I thought I heard someone knocking at the gate. Let's go see who it is."

When the people went to the gate, who did they find? "Peter!" they all shouted.

It was hard for Peter's friends to believe that it was he, alive and well. It all seemed so impossible. But God likes to do impossible things. And Rhoda was the first to believe that He did.


WHAT DO YOU THINK?

*What this story teaches:* God does impossible things for those who believe.

1. What impossible things did God do in this story? Was it hard for Peter to believe those impossible things? Was it hard for Peter's friends?

2. Did Rhoda believe in Peter's impossible escape? Do you think she believed more quickly than Peter's other friends?

# The Impossible Mr. Crabberry

"Well, what do you think?" the Sunday school teacher asked as soon as she had finished reading about Peter's impossible escape from prison. "Can God do impossible things?"

"Sure," said Maxi. "He can do anything."

"Aw, I don't know," Pookie argued. "There must be something He can't do."

"Like what?" Mini asked. "Just think of one thing God can't do."

Pookie thought for a moment. Then he chuckled. "Yeah," he said. "Bring old Mr. Crabberry to our Sunday school so he can learn about Jesus."

Maxi gulped and Mini looked down at the floor. That did seem impossible, even for God.

"This could be a very interesting test of what we really believe," said the teacher. "How many of us honestly believe that God *can't* do this?"

Pookie started to put his hand up. But when he saw that no else did, he quickly slipped his down.

"Good," said the teacher. "We all believe God *can* do it. Now let's talk about a way God can use *you* to do it."

"*Us?*" Maxi and Mini and their friends all shouted.

"I thought God was going to do this," said Pookie. "Old Mr. Crabberry is so mean that he would roast us alive."

The others laughed when Pookie said that. Mr. Crabberry was mean, but he wasn't that mean.

"How would you like God to do this?" asked the teacher.

"Oh, I don't know," Pookie answered. "Just zap him, I suppose."

"Maybe God will zap him," said the teacher. "But He always does His zapping through His people. So where do we start?"

"I figure we have to start by praying for him," said Maxi. "That way we can start working with God on this project."

"Good," said the teacher. "We'll do that right now."

One by one, Maxi and Mini and their friends prayed for Mr. Crabberry. By the time they had finished, they began to get excited about their plans to get Mr. Crabberry to Sunday school.

After Sunday dinner, Maxi and Mini decided they would visit Mr. Crabberry and ask him to come with them the following Sunday. "Maybe all he needs is for someone to ask him," Maxi suggested.

But when Maxi and Mini cut across his lawn to ring his doorbell, Mr. Crabberry opened his door and shouted at them. "Get off my grass, you urchins," he shouted. "Can't you see you're mashing it down? I can't even mow it!"

"It is long," Maxi whispered to Mini. "I wonder why."

"Let's ask him," said Mini.

"May we talk with you?" Maxi asked Mr. Crabberry.

"Oh, all right," said Mr. Crabberry. "But just for a minute."

"Good," said Mini. "Why don't you cut your grass?"

"*Mini!*" said Maxi. "Shh."

"That's all right," said Mr. Crabberry. "It's no secret. My lawnmower is broken and I can't afford to fix it, and I've got a bad heart and can't push my old one around. Now you know. Your minute is up and your nosy question is answered, so you can go on home now."

Maxi and Mini talked all the way home about Mr. Crabberry. They had almost forgotten about taking him to Sunday school. Now they were talking about his lawn.

"Maxi, what can we do?" Mini asked.

"Mow his lawn for him tomorrow afternoon," said Maxi.

And that is exactly what Maxi and Mini did. But as soon as they started to mow his lawn, Mr. Crabberry opened the door and shouted at them. "Hey! What are you doing?" he called.

"Mowing your lawn for you," Maxi answered.

"Stop!" shouted Mr. Crabberry. "I don't have any money to pay you."

"We wouldn't take it if you did," said Maxi and Mini. "This is our love gift to you."

Mr. Crabberry stood on the front porch and watched quietly while Maxi and Mini mowed the lawn. At last they were finished.

"All done!" said Maxi. "We'll be on our way now."

"Wait!" said Mr. Crabberry. "You can't leave now. How about some ice cream?"

"Why?" Mr. Crabberry asked as he and Maxi and Mini sat at a table on his patio. "Why did you do it?"

"Well, we decided that Jesus loves you," said Mini. "And we love Jesus. So, that means we must love you, too. And when we love people, we do things to help them."

Mr. Crabberry was very quiet for a moment. "You're the first person who has said that to me in many years," he said. "Long ago when my wife was living, she was a Sunday school teacher. She always wanted me to go with her, but I never did. If only I knew of a good Sunday school and church, I would go."

Maxi and Mini stared at each other. They could hardly believe it. It was impossible! God had answered their prayer and with their help done the impossible.

"We'll come by for you at 9:30 next Sunday morning," they both said, clapping their hands. Then they ran home to call their Sunday school teacher to tell her the good news.

LET'S TALK ABOUT THIS

*What this story teaches:* We can pray and help God do impossible things today, just as He did impossible things through others in Bible times.

1. Can you think of anything God cannot do?
2. Think of ways you can help God do some impossible things. What should you do before you start working for Him? What did Maxi and Mini and their friends do?
3. Sometimes God says yes; sometimes He says no. If God says no to some impossible thing you want to do for Him, remember that He has a good reason. Accept it and try something else for Him.

# TOWARD A NEW LAND

# The Promised Land
## NUMBERS 13—14

"Trust the Lord!" Moses told the people of Israel.

"We will!" the people answered.

But the people broke their promises. When they reached the Red Sea, they did not trust the Lord to take care of them.

Then the Lord led them across on dry ground.

"Trust the Lord!" Moses told the people again.

"We will!" the people said.

But while the people waited for Moses to come down from Mount Sinai, they forgot about trusting the Lord. They built a golden calf and worshiped it.

Then the Lord brought Moses down with the laws of God, written by the finger of God.

"Trust the Lord!" Moses told the people again and again.

"We will!" the people repeated each time. But they often turned away from the Lord and refused to trust Him.

At last Moses led the people to the edge of the land God had promised to give them. The people were excited as they thought about entering the land, building homes, planting fields and vineyards, and raising their families in this wonderful new place.

"But there are people living in our Promised Land," Moses told the Israelites. "We must learn more about them so we can drive them out."

Moses chose twelve brave men to go through the land as spies. "Find out all you can about the people and their cities," said Moses. "Learn what the crops are and how we can conquer this land."

The twelve spies went into the land. For forty days they went everywhere, looking at the cities and their walls, the people, the crops, and ways they could conquer the land. At last they came back to the camp of Israel.

"It is a rich country," some spies said. "Look at the grapes we brought back."

The spies held up a bunch of grapes. It was so large that two men had to carry it on a pole resting on their shoulders.

"But the people are giants," said other spies. "And their cities have great walls. We can never conquer this land."

Some of the people began to cry and say bad things about Moses. They had walked across the desert for two years, and now they couldn't go into the land of promise.

"Wait!" said two of the spies, whose names were Joshua and Caleb. "The land is rich. The people are great, and their cities have big walls. But God is with us, and He will help us conquer the land."

"Trust Him!" said Moses.

"Trust Him!" said the two men.

"No!" said the people. "We want to go home to Egypt. We want to be slaves again in that land where we had food to eat."

God was angry when He heard this. Time after time He had done wonderful things for these people. He had brought them through many dangers to the Promised Land. He had promised to go with them and help them conquer it. But the people would not listen.

"Kill Moses! Kill Joshua and Caleb!" the people shouted. Some picked up big stones to throw at God's leaders.

But before they could throw one stone, God came to the tabernacle, His tent home, in a blaze of glorious light. Then He spoke to the people through Moses.

"You do not trust Me," He said. "So you must wander through this wilderness for forty years. You will never enter the Promised Land. I will give it instead to your children, and they may go in."

The people were sorry now. But it was too late. Because they had refused to trust God, He refused to help them conquer the Promised Land. They would stay in the wilderness until they died.

WHAT DO YOU THINK?

*What this story teaches:* We should accept God's good gifts, for to refuse them will lead us into trouble.

1. Why was God angry at His people? What had they done?

2. Why did God refuse to let His people go into the Promised Land? What does this teach you about trusting God?

32

# No Strings

"But Poppi, don't you think Mini and I will be bored tonight?" Maxi asked.

Poppi smiled. "I don't think so," he answered. "Several people have heard the evangelist who is speaking at our church tonight, and they think he will be interesting to you as well as to Mommi and me."

Maxi puckered up his face. He wasn't so sure, but if Mommi and Poppi said he and Mini should go, they would go.

As soon as the Muffin Family arrived at church, who should they see but Pookie and BoBo. "Hey," said Pookie. "May we sit with you and your family, Maxi?"

The Muffins were glad to have Pookie and BoBo sit with them. Before long, one of Mini's friends joined them, too.

The music was great, and Maxi whispered that to Pookie about four times before Mommi shushed him. By the time the evangelist stood up, Maxi was really glad that he had come.

"I have a special gift for someone under twelve," the evangelist said. As soon as he said that, Maxi and Mini and their friends sat up straight. They listened carefully as the evangelist went on.

"There are no strings attached to this gift," said the evangelist. "The first person under twelve to come up here may have it." Then the evangelist held up a five-dollar bill.

Pookie looked at Maxi, and Maxi looked at BoBo. "There's a catch somewhere," they whispered. "People just don't give five-dollar bills away without a catch."

"But he said there are no strings," Maxi whispered.

"What are 'no strings'?" Mini whispered to Mommi.

Mommi didn't want to add to the whispering, but she thought it was important for Mini to know. "That means you just accept a gift without owing anything to the person who gives it to you," she said softly.

"No strings," said the evangelist again. "Who will be the first to come and get it?"

But Pookie and BoBo and Maxi sat frozen in their places. They all wanted to rush up and get the five-dollar bill. But they were afraid there were strings attached to it. They were afraid the evangelist might ask them to do something strange when they got up there.

Mini could hardly believe her eyes. She had expected Maxi or one of his friends to jump up first. When they didn't, she stood up and walked to the front of the church.

"Good!" said the evangelist. "I'm glad this young lady believes me when I say there are no strings. Here you are, young lady. It's all yours, just for the taking."

Maxi and Pookie and BoBo gulped as Mini walked back with the five-dollar bill. She really didn't have to do anything but take it. It was hers.

"When God gives us something, there are no strings attached to the gift," said the evangelist. "Like the time He wanted to give a special land to His people."

Maxi and Mini listened carefully. They had just read about this in their new *Over Buttonwood Bridge* book last night. And they remembered how the spies had told the people of Israel not to take this special land that God offered. The spies had said there were strings on God's gift, so they couldn't receive it.

"I'm glad we came," said Mini when the service ended.

"Because you received the five-dollar bill?" asked Poppi.

"Partly," said Mini. "But mostly because I will always remember now to accept God's gifts because they have no strings on them."

Then Mini thought for a moment. "I have a gift for the Muffin Family," she said. "There are no strings attached. Will you take it?"

"Yeah!" said Maxi.

"Good," said Mini. "If it's OK with Mommi and Poppi, we'll buy chocolate sundaes for the whole family with the five-dollar bill. And let's also invite the evangelist to go with us!"

"Think he will?" asked Maxi.

"Sure," said Mini. "We'll just tell him there are no strings attached to the chocolate sundaes."

LET'S TALK ABOUT THIS

*What this story teaches:* We should accept God's good gifts, trusting Him to give us what is best for us.

1. What did the evangelist mean when he said that God's gifts have no strings attached to them?

2. What are some of God's good gifts that He offers us? How should we receive them?

3. Will you remember to thank God for his good gifts?

# When The Walls Fell Down
JOSHUA 6

"Look at those walls," some people of Israel said. "How can we ever go over them to conquer Jericho?"

"God will help us," said Joshua. "We must trust Him to help us conquer Jericho."

The people wondered how God would help them conquer such a great city with such large walls. But they knew that they must do exactly what God told them.

One day God told Joshua what the people must do to conquer Jericho. How strange it must have seemed to the people. But they were going to do what God said no matter how strange it seemed.

On the first day, the people marched around the city of Jericho. The soldiers went first, then seven priests who blew on trumpets. Next came some priests who carried the golden chest in which the Ten Commandments were placed. After them came more soldiers. They marched around the city once, then went home.

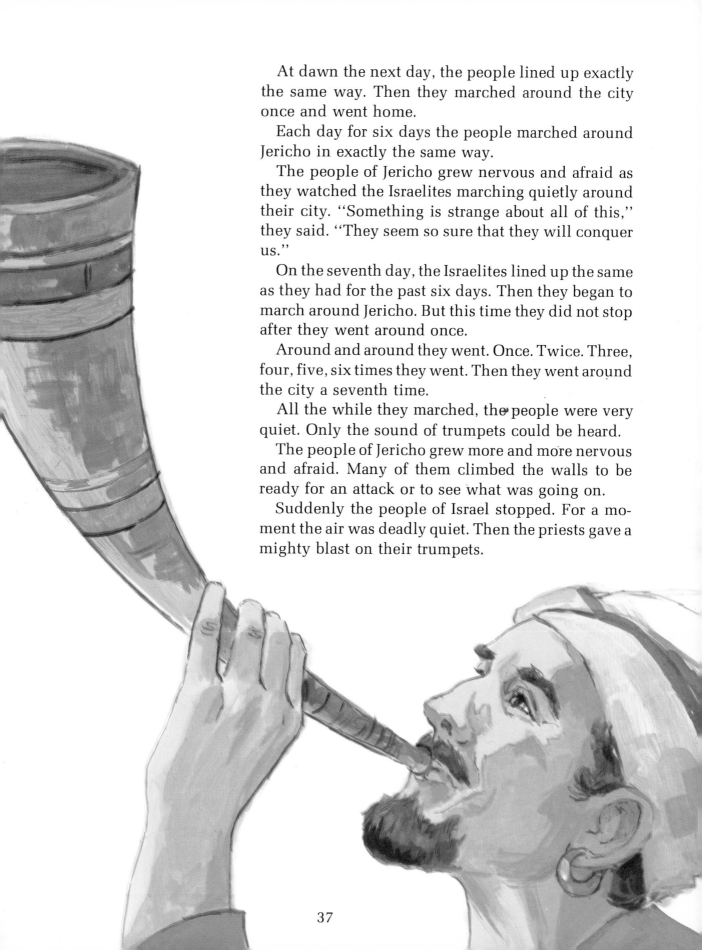

At dawn the next day, the people lined up exactly the same way. Then they marched around the city once and went home.

Each day for six days the people marched around Jericho in exactly the same way.

The people of Jericho grew nervous and afraid as they watched the Israelites marching quietly around their city. "Something is strange about all of this," they said. "They seem so sure that they will conquer us."

On the seventh day, the Israelites lined up the same as they had for the past six days. Then they began to march around Jericho. But this time they did not stop after they went around once.

Around and around they went. Once. Twice. Three, four, five, six times they went. Then they went around the city a seventh time.

All the while they marched, the people were very quiet. Only the sound of trumpets could be heard.

The people of Jericho grew more and more nervous and afraid. Many of them climbed the walls to be ready for an attack or to see what was going on.

Suddenly the people of Israel stopped. For a moment the air was deadly quiet. Then the priests gave a mighty blast on their trumpets.

"Shout! The Lord has given Jericho to us!" Joshua called out to his people.

The people of Israel shouted so loud that it sounded like great thunder rolling across the plains toward the city. Suddenly the mighty walls of Jericho began to tremble. Then with a mighty roar, they tumbled outward, away from the city.

"Attack!" shouted Joshua.

The soldiers of Israel rushed into the city and captured it. There was hardly a fight, for the people of Jericho were so frightened that they tried to run away.

"We conquered mighty Jericho!" some soldiers shouted.

"No," said others. "God conquered mighty Jericho, for we trusted Him to help us."

It was true, for without God's help, how could the people of Israel have gone over those mighty walls?

WHAT DO YOU THINK?

*What this story teaches:* God can do great things through us if we obey Him completely.

1. How might this story have been different if the people had marched around Jericho eight times instead of seven? Or if they had laughed and joked as they walked around instead of marching quietly?

2. What does this story teach you about obeying God completely? Is anything too hard for God when we do things His way?

# Pink Geraniums

"Mommi, may I go with you for your art lesson?" Mini Muffin asked.

"I suppose so," said Mommi. "But won't you be bored? There isn't much to do at Michael Angelo's studio."

"Oh, I'll find something to do," said Mini. "But I love to watch you and Mr. Angelo paint. OK? Please, Mommi?"

"Oh, all right," Mommi said. "I'm sure Mike won't mind."

Mommi put her brushes and paints and other art supplies in her case and headed for Michael Angelo's studio, with Mini bouncing along at her side. "What are you going to paint today?" Mini asked.

"We're painting flowers now," said Mommi. "They can really be beautiful when I follow Mike's instructions."

Mini puckered up her mouth. That didn't sound like fun. She thought an artist should do what she wanted to do instead of following someone's instructions.

"Why do you have to do what he says?" Mini asked, almost angrily. "Why can't you do your painting the way you want to do it?"

Mommi laughed. "I'm only a beginner," she said. "Mike is an expert. He's a very talented painter. Until I'm much better, he will tell me how to mix colors to get the special effects we want and how to do many of the things that will make me a better artist."

Mini was quiet for almost two minutes. She was thinking about mixing paints. That would be fun!

Mini was still thinking about mixing paints when she and Mommi walked into Mr. Angelo's studio. But she was surprised when she saw how many tubes of paint there were.

"How do you know what to mix?" Mini asked.

Mr. Angelo laughed. "It takes a long time to learn to be a good painter," he said. "Your Mommi is doing fine, but she still can use a little help."

"Good, then I will help her," said Mini. "May I help mix some paints, please?"

Mr. Angelo thought for a moment. "Why not?" he said. "That way you and your Mommi can do it together."

Mini watched as Mr. Angelo laid a number of tubes of paint on a tray. "Usually I mix certain colors together until I see the exact color I want," he said. "But I'll tell you how much of each to put in, so you follow my instructions completely."

Mini puckered her mouth again. Now he was trying to take the fun out of mixing paint! She was sure of that.

"OK, first you will mix the nice, soft pink for your Mommi's geraniums," he said. "So put in two parts of this red and three parts of white. Then add just a tiny touch of blue."

Mr. Angelo hurried away to set up an easel. Mini was confused, but she didn't want to ask Mr. Angelo again. She was afraid he might not let her mix more paint if she told him she was confused.

Mini picked up the tube of red paint and squeezed two parts onto the tray. "There, I'm sure that's right," she said to herself. "But what else did he say?"

Mini was sure he had said something about blue, so she picked up the blue tube and squeezed out three parts of it. "And he said white," she whispered.

As soon as Mini squeezed a tiny touch of white into the paint, she mixed it and gave it to Mommi.

Mommi looked puzzled. "That doesn't look right for geraniums," she said with a frown. "But if that's what Mike wants, I'll use it."

Just when Mommi began to put the purple paint on the board, Mr. Angelo came by. "Yek!" he shouted. "Who ever heard of purple geraniums?"

"It—it's all my fault, not Mommi's," said Mini. "I got mixed up and didn't remember your instructions."

"Yes, yes, I see that," said Mr. Angelo. "Now watch the difference when we mix exactly what we should."

Mini watched carefully as Mr. Angelo mixed the paints together into a pretty, soft pink. Then he picked up a brush, and within a few minutes a beautiful pink geranium began to appear on the board.

"Oh," whispered Mini. "It's beautiful!"

Mommi smiled. "See what wonderful things can happen when we do things exactly the way we should?" she asked. "Just like the people of Israel when they marched around Jericho!"

"The story you read last night," said Mini. "I remember! They followed God's instructions exactly, didn't they?"

"Yes, and God did some wonderful things through them when they did," said Mommi.

"I'm glad I came to Mr. Angelo's studio today," said Mini. "I learned about mixing paint, and I learned about following God's instructions."

"That's better than painting pink geraniums," said Mommi.

LET'S TALK ABOUT THIS

*What this story teaches:* Wonderful and beautiful things happen when we obey God.

1. What happened when Mini mixed the paints the wrong way? What did that do to Mommi's painting?

2. What did Mini learn about following God's instructions?

3. Where do you find God's instructions for you? Think about this as you read your Bible today.

# WOMEN WHO DARED

# Deborah and Jael:
JUDGES 4–5

# Dare to Be a Leader

"Take ten thousand men and go to Mount Tabor to fight the Canaanites," Deborah said to General Barak one day.

"But they have nine hundred iron chariots on their side," Barak argued.

"And you have God on your side," said Deborah.

For twenty years the people of Israel had served King Jabin and his Canaanites. God had let this happen because Israel had not served Him. At last the people of Israel cried out for God to help, and God said He would.

At that time, the people of Israel had no king to lead them. Instead, Deborah had been chosen to lead the people. Each day she sat beneath a palm tree, where people came to have her settle disagreements between them. They knew that God helped her decide what was best.

On this day, Deborah had called for General Barak to come to see her, and she gave him the message that God wanted him to fight the Canaanites. "I will go if you will go also and help lead our army," said Barak.

"I will go," said Deborah. "But you must know now that General Sisera of the Canaanites will be defeated by a woman, not by you."

Before long, Barak gathered the ten thousand men of Israel and set up camp at Mount Tabor. General Sisera of the Canaanites heard about this and ordered his men to go into battle with their nine hundred iron chariots.

"God will give you victory today!" Deborah said to Barak. "Go out to meet Sisera."

So instead of waiting at Mount Tabor, Barak and his men went to fight General Sisera. Sisera was sure that he would win easily with his nine hundred chariots. But Sisera did not know that God was helping Deborah and Barak.

Soon General Sisera realized that he could not win this battle. Afraid for his life, he ran away.

Sisera ran far from the battleground, looking for a place to hide. When he reached the tent of a woman named Jael, he thought he was safe, for Jael's people had been friendly to the Canaanites.

"Hurry! Come in here!" Jael shouted to Sisera. Sisera hurried inside and crawled under a rug to hide.

"May I have some water?" Sisera asked.

"I will give you something better," said Jael. So she gave him some warm milk to drink.

"Watch at the doorway of your tent for enemies," Sisera said.

It wasn't long before Sisera went into a deep sleep. The warm milk and the strain of battle were too much! He could not stay awake.

When Jael knew that Sisera was sleeping, she went quietly to him with a hammer and a tent peg. She would help Israel's people in their fight against this evil man and his people.

Jael lifted the hammer and drove the tent peg into Sisera's head while he slept. When Jael showed Barak what she had done, Barak remembered what Deborah had told him. "Sisera will be defeated by a woman, not by you."

Barak must have thought much that day about Deborah and Jael. Chariots, generals, and fierce warriors had gone to battle against each other. But the leaders who had taken Israel to victory were Deborah and Jael.

WHAT DO YOU THINK?

*What this story teaches:* God uses leaders for His work who dare to do what He wants.

1. What does this story tell you about courage? How did Deborah show courage? How did Barak?

2. Does it take more courage to be a leader than a follower?

# Summer Parade

"That was a good story about Deborah," said Mini. "I wish I had her courage."

"Don't you have her courage?" asked Poppi as he laid down their new Muffin Family book, *Over Buttonwood Bridge*.

"I don't know," said Mini as she shrugged her shoulders.

Mommi smiled. "I think Mini would have that kind of courage for God if she really thought God wanted her to do something special," she said. "But we had all better get ready if we want to see the parade and the mayor's ceremonies."

Mini and Maxi clapped their hands and ran to get ready. This would be a fun parade. And they were sure that it would even be fun to hear what the mayor had to say about their city.

The parade *was* fun! Pop's Sweet Shop had a beautiful float. "Just like a big chocolate sundae," said Maxi, licking his lips.

"And look at the float from Brown's Hardware Store," said Mini. "How did they ever make those e-nor-mous hammers, saws, and things?"

"They planted little hammer and saw seeds and grew big ones," said Maxi, with a mischievous grin.

"Maxi!" Mini said, trying to frown and grin at the same time.

Maxi and Mini clapped their hands and shouted as they watched the fire engines pass by, and then the bands and scout troops.

At last the parade was over and it was time for the mayor to say a few words. The Muffin Family found a place near the front of the crowd and listened carefully as the mayor told of the things he would like to see happen in their city.

"What we need in our city is a great evangelistic campaign," Poppi whispered. "We need all our churches to join together and ask God to do great things and bring many to Christ."

"Why doesn't the mayor say that?" Mini whispered to Poppi.

"He would like such a thing to happen," said Poppi. "But he can't stand up in a mixed crowd like this and say so."

"But who can say so?" asked Mini.

"I don't know," said Poppi.

The mayor ended his speech and looked out across the crowd in front of him. "I'm going to do something different," he said. "I'm going to ask some of you to come up here and tell what you would like to see happen in this city."

One by one, the mayor called some people up to the microphone to speak. There was the librarian. She thought some summer reading programs would be good. Everyone clapped.

The fire chief thought some home fire drills would help. And the police chief said more people should make their homes burglar resistant.

"Now I'd like to hear from some of our young people," said the mayor. First he called for a teenager who was standing near the platform. Then a junior high young person. They wanted more vacation time from school.

"And now what about this young lady?" the mayor asked, pointing at Mini.

Mini gulped. She looked at Poppi and Mommi. They smiled. "Tell him how to run the city," Poppi whispered.

Mini walked to the microphone and the people clapped. Then they waited to hear what a young girl would say the city needed.

"I would like to see our city have a big evangelistic campaign," said Mini. "Wouldn't it be great if our churches could join together to pray and ask God to bring many to Christ?"

A few people clapped their hands. Then more joined in until there were hundreds of people clapping for Mini.

"Seems to me this young lady has given a very important speech," said the mayor. "Since she has had the courage to say those things, I appoint her as chairman of a committee to organize such a campaign. Of course, I hope she will ask her pastor and family to work with her."

"Just like Deborah!" said Poppi as Mini came down to be with the family.

LET'S TALK ABOUT THIS

*What this story teaches:* We should speak for God with courage and let Him use us to lead others.

1. What did Poppi mean when he said, "Just like Deborah"?

2. What do you think Mini did about the Mayor's appointment? What do you think happened in Mini's city?

3. Think about Mini the next time you are afraid to do something special for God. That may come earlier than you think!

49

# Abigail: Dare to Be a Peacemaker
## 1 SAMUEL 25

King Saul was very angry at David. Everyone said better things about David than they did about King Saul.

"David is a great warrior!"

"David saved our nation from the Philistines!"

"David is such a good person!"

"David! David! David!" Saul shouted. "Next they will want to make him king instead of me."

The king was troubled about this so much that he tried to kill David. So David ran away and hid in the wilderness. Soon other men joined him there. They knew that God was with David and would some day make him king.

More and more men came to live with David and help protect him from Saul. Before long there were six hundred men with him.

David and his men did not have gardens and fields and vineyards in the wilderness, so they had to get their food from farmers and shepherds who wanted to help them. But this wasn't always easy.

For some time, David and his men had camped near the home of a wealthy man named Nabal. When Nabal's shepherds went into the fields with their sheep, David and his men protected them. When Nabal's men went to the fields to plow and to plant their seed, David's men kept enemies from hurting them.

"Perhaps Nabal will give us some food," David said to his men one day. So David sent ten of his men to talk with Nabal.

"Why are you bothering me?" Nabal complained.

"David needs food for his men," the young men answered. "Will you give him some?"

"No!" Nabal shouted. "Why should I give him food? There are too many people begging for food today. Now get out of here!"

David was very angry when his men told him what had happened. "Put on your swords and we will teach Nabal a lesson!" David shouted.

But while David and his men were preparing to fight, a young man on Nabal's farm went to see Abigail, Nabal's wife. "David sent men here to ask for food," the young man said. "But Nabal was rude and angry. These men have helped us many times. Now they may turn against us and kill us all."

Abigail did not want trouble. She knew that Nabal should have helped David and his men. So she ordered some of Nabal's men to put food on some donkeys and go with her to meet David.

"I'm sorry that my husband, Nabal, was such a foolish person with you," she told David, bowing down before him. "But you must not hurt Nabal, for that would only hurt you."

David could see what a wonderful woman Abigail was, not at all like Nabal. "Thank you for being a peacemaker," said David. "I might have killed some of your people. But I will not do that now."

Later, when Nabal died, Abigail became David's wife. And David never forgot that wonderful day when she had been a peacemaker and kept him from killing a foolish man.

WHAT DO YOU THINK?

*What this story teaches:* God will bless the work of peacemakers, for He loves for us to be at peace with one another.

1. How were Nabal and Abigail different? Was Nabal a peacemaker? What did Abigail do that made her a peacemaker?

2. Why does God bless the work of peacemakers?

# Chief Broken Arrow

"Pookie, isn't this going to be a great Indian campfire tonight?" Maxi asked.

"Yeah, I suppose," said Pookie. "But I just hope BoBo isn't there."

Maxi frowned. "Are you and BoBo still angry at each other?" he asked.

Pookie nodded. He was a little ashamed to admit it, but it was true.

"Chief Ray says you two boys are keeping God from doing His best work here at camp," Maxi reminded Pookie. "God could do some great things at camp this week if you two would get things straightened out."

Pookie hung his head. Chief Ray had told him that. He had told BoBo that, too. So why didn't BoBo do something about it? Why did he have to?

That night when Maxi came to the Indian campfire, he noticed that Pookie was sitting on one side and BoBo on the other side. Maxi decided he would not sit with either one, for he didn't want to take sides in their argument. Instead, he sat with some other boys in the middle.

While everyone sang, Maxi looked at Pookie and then at BoBo. Once or twice each one looked at Maxi, but then looked quickly away. Maxi knew it was because he had talked with both of them and urged them to make up.

At last it was time for the closing part of the campfire, when each boy brought an arrow forward and pushed the point into the ground in front of the fire. As he did this, he was to think about something special he would do for God.

One by one the boys brought their arrows forward and quietly pushed them into the ground before the campfire. Then each boy stood by his arrow for a moment before returning to his place around the fire.

Maxi watched as Pookie went forward. Then, after several other boys had taken their turns, BoBo went forward with his arrow. But still neither boy looked at the other. At last it was time for Maxi to go to the campfire with his arrow.

Maxi walked forward slowly and pushed his arrow point into the ground. Then he stood beside his arrow. Maxi was very quiet as he thought about something special he would do for God.

Suddenly Maxi pulled his arrow from the ground and turned around to face the other boys. Everyone said "ooh" as Maxi broke his arrow in two.

"What is he doing?" one of the boys whispered.

"I don't know," another whispered back.

Maxi walked slowly over to BoBo and stood before him without saying a word. Then Maxi slowly stretched out his hand and gave BoBo one half of his arrow.

BoBo looked puzzled until he saw Maxi walking over to Pookie. Slowly, without a word, Maxi stretched out his hand and gave the other half of his arrow to Pookie.

Pookie gulped as Maxi quietly went back to his place and sat down. Then Pookie looked over at BoBo. He wasn't even sure what their argument had been now. He was ashamed if he and BoBo had kept God from doing His best work at camp.

Pookie got up and started walking toward BoBo. He would ask BoBo to forgive him, no matter what BoBo would do. But before he could reach BoBo's place, he saw BoBo get up and walk toward him.

"I'm sorry!" they both said as they met in the middle before the campfire. "Forgive me!"

Later, when Chief Ray gave the invitation for boys to come forward to ask Jesus into their hearts, six boys left their places and came up. It was the first time that had happened all week.

After the campfire was over, Maxi started walking toward his cabin. But he had not gone far before he felt a big hand on his shoulder.

"Blessed are the peacemakers, Chief Broken Arrow," a voice said. "Here's a new arrow to replace your broken one."

Maxi smiled as he took the new arrow from Chief Ray's hand. "Thanks," he whispered. "Maybe I can do better at archery tomorrow with this one."

"Well, you hit the bullseye tonight!" said Chief Ray. "And with a broken arrow, at that."

LET'S TALK ABOUT THIS

*What this story teaches:* We can help God do His work better when we are peacemakers, helping people forgive one another.

1. How was Maxi a peacemaker like Abigail?
2. Think of a way you can be a peacemaker for God this next week. Will you? And will you ask God to help you?

# Mary: Dare to Obey

### LUKE 1:26-38

"Mary," a voice said softly.

Mary was surprised and afraid to hear a voice speaking to her. She was alone in her room, praying to God.

Mary jumped up and looked around the room. Then she caught her breath. There on the other side of the room was an angel. It was not only an angel, but one of the chief angels of all heaven.

56

"Who . . . who are you?" Mary asked softly. "What do you want?"

"I am the angel Gabriel," the angel answered. "I have good news for you."

Mary grew more frightened as the angel spoke. Why would an angel visit her? She was just a poor girl of Nazareth. She had heard about angel visits to great kings and prophets. And she had heard how an angel had visited the priest Zacharias in the Temple to tell him about a special son that he and Elizabeth would have. But why would an angel visit her?

"You must not be afraid," said the angel. "God has chosen you to do something special for Him."

"Me?" Mary whispered. "What special work could I do for Him?"

"God wants you to have a baby boy," said the angel. "This baby will be the Messiah, the Savior of the world."

Mary could hardly speak. Her people had prayed for hundreds of years for the Messiah to come. They had told of the wonderful way that God would honor some woman by letting her be the mother of the Messiah.

Then Mary remembered. "But Joseph and I are not married yet," she said. "How can I have a baby?"

"This will not be Joseph's baby," said the angel. "The Holy Spirit will come to you. This baby will be God's Son."

Mary began to think of many things. What would she say to Joseph? What would Joseph do? Would he understand? Would he break their engagement when he learned that she would have a baby? Being the mother of the Messiah was a great honor. But it could also cause her many problems. Should she say yes to the angel?

"I will do whatever God wants me to do," Mary said.

Then Mary must have prayed something like this: "Thank You, Lord, for letting me do Your special work, no matter what it might cost me."

WHAT DO YOU THINK?

*What this story teaches:* God wants us to obey Him and do His special work, no matter what it may cost us.

1. What special work did God want Mary to do? In what special way did God let her know about this?

2. In what ways could this special work have hurt Mary? What did Mary decide to do about it?

# The Tea Set

"I'm so glad you have no school this afternoon, Mini," said Mommi. "I have something you can do for me."

Mini looked as sour as a green apple when Mommi said that. "I have one afternoon off and I have to work," she grumbled under her breath. But she didn't say that to Mommi.

"What can I do for you?" Mini asked.

"I don't like to ask you to do this," said Mommi. "But I really need your help. Poor Mrs. Friggles can't get out to the store much, and I've made a dozen plastic containers of stew for her. If you could put them in your wagon and take them to her, I would appreciate it."

Mini was still looking glum when she loaded her wagon with the plastic containers, which Mommi had put into two bags. "Did you have something important to do this afternoon?" Mommi asked softly.

"Well, I wanted so much to go to Maria's house," said Mini. "She just got a miniature china tea set for her birthday, and it's just like the old ones you probably had when you were a girl."

"Is it that old?" Mommi asked.

"Oh, no," said Mini. "It's new. But it's made to look like a real antique."

"I'm sorry," said Mommi. "I can't take the stew, and Mrs. Friggles needs some for dinner tonight. Poppi won't be home in time to take it over, and Maxi is at baseball practice. So you see, Mrs. Friggles needs you."

"Then I'll go," said Mini, "even though I'd rather play. I'll just have to wait to play with Maria's tea set. And Mommi, sometime you can get me a set like that for Christmas or my birthday. I'd love to have one."

Mommi smiled. She thought of the tea set as Mini went down the sidewalk with her wagonload of stew. Mommi remembered how she had played with a set like that when she was a little girl.

Mini was still feeling glum when she pulled her wagon up to Mrs. Friggles's door. *This is halfway across town,* she thought. *By the time I get home, it will be too late to play with Maria.*

Mrs. Friggles was so glad to see Mini. "Your Mommi is sweet to think of me," she said. "It's hard for me to do things anymore. So it's quite a help when someone does something special like this for me."

Mini carried the plastic containers into Mrs. Friggles's house and helped her put them in her refrigerator and freezer. She was almost ready to leave when she noticed how different Mrs. Friggles's house looked from her own. Mini began to think of the difference. Mommi kept her house so sparkling clean, and this house was so—well, dirty.

"Who does your housework?" Mini asked.

"It is a bit dirty," said Mrs. Friggles. "I'm sorry. I don't have anyone to do it for me, and I'm not well enough to do it myself."

Mini thought for a moment. "Do you have a vacuum cleaner?" she asked.

"Of course," said Mrs. Friggles. "I keep it in the closet over there."

"Well, first I'll call Mommi and tell her I'll be home about dinner time," said Mini. "Then I'll help you tidy things a little."

Mrs. Friggles watched from her chair as Mini vacuumed the rug carefully from one end to the other. Then Mini washed the dishes in the kitchen sink and cleaned all the furniture tops. Mini grunted and groaned a little as she sprayed each window with glass cleaner and rubbed it until it sparkled. Then at last Mini flopped down in a big chair next to Mrs. Friggles.

"Whew!" she said. "That's about all I can do in one day."

"Bless you, child," said Mrs. Friggles. "You did more work here this afternoon than I could do in the next two months."

"Good, and I'll stop some other time and help you again," said Mini. "Now I'd better scoot home."

"Just one more thing you can do for me," said Mrs. Friggles.

Mini was sure she was too tired to do one more thing, but she would do it anyway. "Open that drawer over there and bring that dark blue box to me," said Mrs. Friggles.

Mini ran to do exactly as Mrs. Friggles said. She was having fun doing special work for her, even though it had cost her the afternoon of play.

When Mini brought the box, Mrs. Friggles smiled and opened it gently. There, inside, was the most beautiful miniature tea set Mini had ever seen. "It was mine when I was a little girl," said Mrs. Friggles. "Now it's an antique. I saved it for many years, hoping I would have a granddaughter to give it to, but I never did. But today you have been a granddaughter to me. It's yours, Mini. I want you to have it."

Mini's heart sang all the way home and when she showed the beautiful tea set to Mommi. She had never thought of Mrs. Friggles giving her something. She had only meant to do a special work for her and Mommi.

LET'S TALK ABOUT THIS

*What this story teaches:* We should do special work for God and others, no matter what it may cost us.

1. What did it cost Mini to obey Mommi and take the stew to Mrs. Friggles? Did she expect any reward for doing this?

2. But what reward did Mini receive? What reward did she receive besides the tea set?

3. Read Mark 12:30-31. What does this story teach about loving God and others?

# THE WEEK WE REMEMBER

# The King Who Rode a Donkey
MATTHEW 21:1-11, 14-17

"Will you do something for Me?" Jesus asked two of His disciples.

"We will do anything for You," they answered.

"Good," said Jesus. "When you go into that little village over there, you will find a donkey tied to a fence. Bring it to Me."

The disciples looked surprised. "But what if someone stops us?" they said. "What if someone tells us we can't take the donkey?"

Jesus smiled. "Tell him I need the donkey," He said. "He will let you bring it to Me."

The disciples walked into the little village and made their way up the narrow street. *How does Jesus know there is a donkey here?* they wondered. *He has not been here for some time. And how does He know the owner will let us take it?*

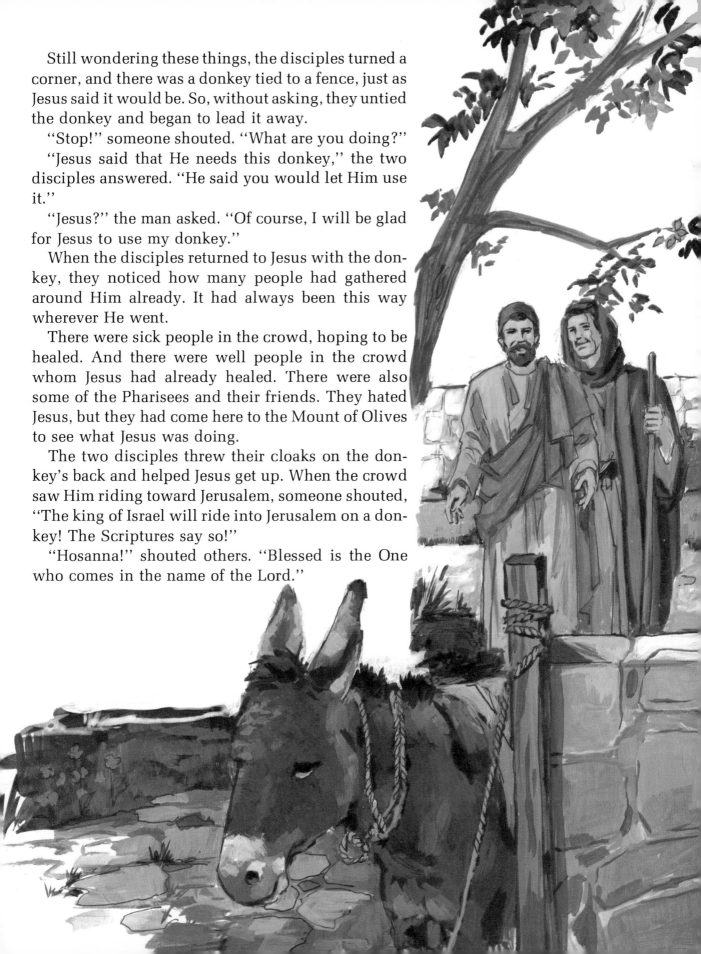

Still wondering these things, the disciples turned a corner, and there was a donkey tied to a fence, just as Jesus said it would be. So, without asking, they untied the donkey and began to lead it away.

"Stop!" someone shouted. "What are you doing?"

"Jesus said that He needs this donkey," the two disciples answered. "He said you would let Him use it."

"Jesus?" the man asked. "Of course, I will be glad for Jesus to use my donkey."

When the disciples returned to Jesus with the donkey, they noticed how many people had gathered around Him already. It had always been this way wherever He went.

There were sick people in the crowd, hoping to be healed. And there were well people in the crowd whom Jesus had already healed. There were also some of the Pharisees and their friends. They hated Jesus, but they had come here to the Mount of Olives to see what Jesus was doing.

The two disciples threw their cloaks on the donkey's back and helped Jesus get up. When the crowd saw Him riding toward Jerusalem, someone shouted, "The king of Israel will ride into Jerusalem on a donkey! The Scriptures say so!"

"Hosanna!" shouted others. "Blessed is the One who comes in the name of the Lord."

Before long the air was filled with shouts of "Hosanna! Hosanna in the highest!"

Someone began to lead the donkey down the Mount of Olives toward Jerusalem. As he did, more and more people began to shout, "Hosanna!"

"What is it?" asked the people who joined the crowd.

"A new king for Israel!" someone answered.

People were excited about the thought of a new king. They had waited for a king to come who would free them from the Romans.

People began to throw their cloaks in front of Jesus. Others cut branches and laid them in His path. Children shouted. Mothers and fathers waved their hands. The air was filled with joy.

But the Pharisees and their friends were not happy. "A new king?" they said angrily. "If Jesus becomes king, He will take our jobs from us."

"Stop those people from saying such things," they demanded of Jesus.

"If I do, the stones will shout praises!" Jesus answered. "The Scriptures, God's Word, said this would happen, so who can stop it?"

Through the gate of Jerusalem the procession went. The people were proclaiming Jesus king. But they did not realize what kind of king He was. He would not free them from the Romans. He would free some from their sins and give them a new life in Him.

WHAT DO YOU THINK?

*What this story teaches:* Jesus does not free us from all our problems, but He does free us from our sins.

1. What kind of king do you think the people expected Jesus to be? What did they expect Him to do?

2. But what kind of king was He? From what does He free people? Which kind of king is better?

67

# The Great Tent Meeting

"Let's get that blanket fastened to your end, Maxi," Pookie called. "The great tent meeting is about to begin."

"Why do you have to be the preacher?" Maxi grumbled.

"Because I called for it first," Pookie answered. "Besides, who else should do it?"

Maxi didn't want to argue about it, so he kept quiet. But he was sure that he could do as well as Pookie.

As soon as the blanket was fastened, Pookie called for all his friends to set up the folding chairs so that the meeting could begin. Then he stood up behind the lettuce-crate pulpit.

"*La*-dees and gen-tul-men!" Pookie began. That seemed like a safe way to begin, although he had never really heard a preacher begin that way.

"The most *won*-derful thing can happen to you today," Pookie went on. "If you will just come up here and become a Christian, your troubles will all be over!"

"That's not true!" Maxi interrupted.

Pookie, BoBo, Mini, and Maria all stared at Maxi. They had never heard anyone interrupt a great tent meeting before. Pookie wasn't sure how to handle this, so he asked a question.

"Why isn't it true?" he said.

"'Cause I'm a Christian, and I've had plenty of problems this last week," Maxi answered.

"Like what?" BoBo asked.

"Like my pet frog died Tuesday," said Maxi. "And Ruff was sick on Thursday. And furthermore, Pookie got to be preacher at this meeting, and I don't think he's very good."

"I have an idea," said Mini. "Let's visit a couple of older Christians we know and ask them."

"Great!" said Pookie. "How about Mrs. Murgatroyd?"

"And Mr. Melloway?" added BoBo.

Within two minutes, the great tent meeting became the great visitation meeting as Maxi, Mini, Pookie, BoBo, and Maria trooped down the street to Mrs. Murgatroyd's house.

"Now, what can I do for you?" Mrs. Murgatroyd asked when her new friends were seated on the floor of her living room.

"We had an argu—er, discussion," said Maxi. "We want to know if Jesus takes away all of a person's problems when he or she becomes a Christian."

Mrs. Murgatroyd smiled. "My oh my," she said. "I've had arthritis so bad for the last few years that I can hardly leave the house. I haven't been able to go to church for the last two months. But I still love Jesus very much."

"Then why doesn't Jesus take your art—arth—whatever it is away?" Pookie asked.

Mrs. Murgatroyd was quiet for a while. "I asked that same question many times," she answered. "Then a few weeks ago I stopped asking and started praying. And do you know what? Ever since I had to stop going to church, I've called many people to ask them to go. Now fifteen people are going because the Lord encouraged me to ask them."

Mini and Maxi and their friends were still thinking about that when they rang Mr. Melloway's doorbell. "Come in! Come in!" he said warmly. "What can I do for you?"

When Maxi and Pookie told about their discussion, Mr. Melloway thought for a moment. "Well, I'm a Christian, and I had a big problem that Jesus never took away," he said. "After my wife died, I was terribly lonely."

"But if you love Jesus and Jesus loves you, why doesn't he take away your problem?" asked BoBo.

"I asked that many times," said Mr. Melloway. "Then one day I stopped asking and began praying. And do you know what?"

"What?" the friends asked.

"Jesus encouraged me to go visit people more lonely than I am," he answered. "So every week I go to the nursing home. Now I have many new friends, and I'm not so lonely anymore."

Before long, Pookie, BoBo, Maxi, Mini, and Maria were back at the great tent meeting. Pookie stood up again behind the lettuce-crate pulpit.

"La-dees and gen-tul-men," he said. "I want to tell you that Jesus can take away your sins. And He will also help you take your problems and make something good happen from them."

"Pookie is a good preacher, isn't he?" Mini whispered.

"Yes, very good!" said Maxi.

LET'S TALK ABOUT THIS

*What this story teaches:* We should ask Jesus to take away our sins and help us make something good come from our problems.

1. What did Maxi and Mini and their friends learn from Mrs. Murgatroyd? From Mr. Melloway?
2. Have you ever wondered why Jesus did not take away all your problems? What should you ask Him to do?

# The Last Supper
## LUKE 22:7-20, 24-30

One by one, Jesus' disciples walked upstairs to the large room in which a table was set. No one said much, for they were all troubled. Jesus had been quiet this evening, and His disciples knew that something strange was about to happen.

One by one, the disciples sat down at the table, each taking the best seat he could find. The seat in the center was left for Jesus.

When Jesus sat down, He looked at His disciples. There was no servant at this supper to wash the disciples' feet before they ate. And there was no servant to wash Jesus' feet, either. Almost every household had someone to wash the guests' feet before they ate.

Quietly, Jesus poured some water into a basin. Then He knelt before each disciple, washing his feet and drying them with a cloth.

The disciples were so shocked that they did not know what to say. When Jesus came to Peter, this disciple would not let Him wash his feet.

"You must not do that," said Peter.

"If I cannot wash your feet, you will have no part in My plans," Jesus answered. So Peter let Jesus wash his feet.

When Jesus was finished, He sat at the table again. "I am your Master and Lord," Jesus said. "But I have done a servant's work for you. Now you must learn to serve each other."

Jesus looked at Judas. "One of you will betray Me," He said. Judas was startled. How did Jesus know? What would He do? The other disciples did not know yet that Judas would betray Jesus to His enemies.

Jesus dipped a piece of bread in a dish and gave it to Judas. "What you are about to do, do quickly," He said.

Judas was frightened now. Quickly he arose and left the room. The other disciples still did not know what was happening. They thought that Judas was going to buy something for Jesus.

Jesus took some bread in His hands, and after He had prayed, He gave it to His disciples. "Take and eat this, for it is My body," He said. "Whenever you do this, remember Me."

Then Jesus took the cup of wine, and after He had prayed, He gave it to His disciples. "Drink this, for it is My blood, which is given for many. Whenever you do this, remember Me."

The disciples could not know the meaning of Jesus' words that night. Nor could they see across the years, when thousands would eat bread and drink a communion cup to remember the death of Jesus.

When the bread was eaten and the cup was finished, Jesus began to sing a hymn. Then all of the disciples began to sing with Him.

At last the greatest supper of all had come to an end. Now Jesus would lead His disciples away from the room to a quiet garden outside the city. Step by step He was moving to the time when He would die for them, and us, to take away our sins.

WHAT DO YOU THINK?

*What this story teaches:* Jesus wants us to remember often how He died for us to take away our sins.

1. What did Jesus do for His disciples that a servant would usually do? How do you think the disciples felt about this?
2. What did He tell His disciples they should do for one another?
3. Why did Jesus call the bread "My body" and the wine "My blood"? When people today take communion, what should they remember about Jesus?

74

# Motto

"What's that on your wall, Mini?"

"That's a motto, Maria."

"What's a motto?"

"It's when someone says something short and good that tells us how to live."

"Where did you get it, Mini?"

"At camp last summer, Maria. My counselor gave it to me and said to look at it each day."

"Why?"

"'Cause it will remind me of Jesus every time I look at it."

"Why?"

"'Cause He's done so much for me."

"Mini, what *has* Jesus done for you?"

"Well, Maria, He died on the cross for my sins. So now I can live forever with Him."

"Wouldn't you live forever if He had not died on the cross, Mini?"

"No, Maria. That was the way God planned for me to live in heaven."

"Then Jesus must have loved you a lot to do that, didn't He?"

"Yes, Maria. And He still loves me."

"Does Jesus love me, too, Mini?"

"Yes, and He died for you, Maria."

"Can I live with Him in heaven forever?"

"If you ask Him to forgive your sins and give you a new life."

"Now?"

"Now!"

"Then can I get a motto like yours for my room?"

"Why do you want that?"

"So I can remember what Jesus did for me, too, Mini."

"Then I'll ask my counselor if she can get one for you."

"Thank you, Mini."

"Thank Jesus, Maria."

"I will, as soon as I ask Him to forgive me and give me a new life."

"Now, Maria?"

"Now, Mini."

LET'S TALK ABOUT THIS

*What this story teaches:* We should remember often how Jesus died to take away our sins and give us new life.

1. Of what did Mini's motto remind her each day? Why is it important to remember these things?

2. What do you do in your church that reminds you that Jesus died to take away your sins and give you new life? Will you thank Him for doing this?

3. Have you asked Jesus to forgive you, take away your sins, and give you a new life? Would you like to do that now?

# One Night in a Garden
## MATTHEW 26:30-56; LUKE 22:39-53

The streets of Jerusalem were quiet and dark as Jesus and His disciples walked toward the Mount of Olives. Through the city gate they went, down the Kidron Valley, then up the side of the mount that took its name from the many olive trees growing on it.

At last Jesus and His friends reached a peaceful grove of olive trees where they often went. It was like a secret meeting place, away from the crowds and the busy city.

As they sat down to talk in this garden called Gethsemane, Jesus spoke quietly to His friends. "Tonight you will all run away from Me," He said.

The disciples stared at Him. How could He say such a thing?

"I'll never run away from You," Peter answered.

"Before the rooster crows tomorrow morning, Peter, you will tell people three times that you do not know Me," Jesus said.

"Never!" Peter said, almost too loud. Then the other disciples joined in. "Never!" they said.

But Jesus had not taken them to Gethsemane to argue. He had gone there to pray. So He took three of His closest friends, Peter, James, and John, and went to the other side of the little garden.

"Stay here and pray with Me," Jesus told the three. "I am so filled with sorrow that I am almost dying."

Then Jesus went a little farther by Himself and prayed. "Father, if You have another way to remove the sins of the world, please do it," Jesus pleaded. "But do what You want, not what I want."

After Jesus prayed awhile, He came back and looked at His three closest friends. They were asleep. "Couldn't you pray with Me for one hour?" He asked. The disciples looked ashamed.

Jesus went off by Himself and began to pray again. But when He returned to His friends, He again found them sleeping.

A third time Jesus went aside to pray. He prayed so earnestly that sweat broke out on Him like great drops of blood. Then in Jesus' moment of greatest need, while His friends slept, an angel came from heaven to comfort Him. Even Jesus needed comfort in a time of great trouble.

At last the time came for the enemy to take Jesus. He could see the flicker of torches as they came across the Kidron Valley toward Gethsemane. Jesus knew that Judas was leading them to His and the disciples' secret hiding place.

"Get up," Jesus said to His friends. "We are about to be betrayed."

Before long, the crowd appeared, with Judas leading them. They carried clubs and torches.

"Whom do you seek?" Jesus asked.

"Jesus," they answered.

"I am Jesus," He told them.

Judas stepped forward and kissed Jesus. "Greetings, Master," he said. That was the signal. The crowd seized Jesus to take Him back to Jerusalem for trial.

Peter was angry by now. He picked up the only sword he could find and swung wildly, cutting off a servant's ear.

"Put that away," Jesus told him. "I could call down an army of angels if I wanted to."

Then Jesus spoke to the crowd. "Let My friends go," He said. But even as He spoke, the disciples ran as frightened sheep do when a wolf attacks. Jesus had said they would run away, and they did. He was alone with the crowd that wanted to kill Him.

WHAT DO YOU THINK?

*What this story teaches:* Even Jesus needed friends and comfort in a time of trouble.

1. How do we know that Jesus needed friends and comfort when trouble came?

2. What did Jesus' friends do when He needed them most? What do you think they should have done? Where else did Jesus get comfort at that time?

80

# No Friends

Maxi was sure that his only friend was the old stump on which he was sitting. He couldn't remember when he had felt more lonely or friendless. He looked up at the stars, just beginning to appear in the late evening sky. They were friendly, but so far away. The warm, yellow light from the windows of his house was friendly, too. But it made him feel even more alone as he thought about the day.

At breakfast, he had asked if Mommi and Poppi could take a little time that evening to play a game or something. Mommi said she had several chores that had to be done. Poppi said he had something important to do and wouldn't be able to play with him.

So when days start bad, they usually just keep on going bad. At least that's what Maxi decided.

At recess time at school, Maxi had wanted to play with Pookie, BoBo, and Tony, but they all whispered and talked together and didn't seem to want to play with Maxi. The same thing happened at lunchtime. By afternoon recess time, Maxi was sure they never wanted to be his friends again.

When Maxi came home from school, Mini made some lame excuse about going uptown to buy some things, so she couldn't play, either. Maxi could see that Mommi was busy with her chores, and Poppi wasn't home from work yet.

"So who else is there?" Maxi had moaned. "Ruff is sleeping in one corner over there, and Tuff is sleeping in another corner. I can't even play with my dog and cat."

Maxi had gone out to the old stump to think and feel sorry for himself. With that many unfriendly friends in one day, Maxi would have been glad for a mouse or chipmunk to squeak at him.

But at the very moment when Maxi felt the most lonely and without friends, he heard a rustling in the leaves behind a clump of bushes. Then he saw the dark form of an animal. The dark form bounded from the bushes and leaped at Maxi.

"Ruff!" Maxi squealed with delight. "Oh, how I need you right now! You *are* my friend, aren't you?"

Maxi was still hugging Ruff when he heard more rustling in the leaves. Then a voice spoke to him.

"It's dinner time, Maxi," said Mini. "Mommi says to find you and tell you it will be ready in five minutes. Come on! I'll race you home."

Maxi, Mini, and Ruff raced for the house as fast as they could go. Just before they reached the house, Tuff joined them in the race. Then all four burst through the kitchen door at about the same time.

"*Surprise! Surprise!*" a chorus of voices sang out.

Maxi could hardly believe his eyes. Pookie, BoBo, Tony, and Maria were there in the kitchen with Mommi and Poppi.

"We have been planning this surprise party for you all day, dummy," said Maxi's friends. "But you kept trying to horn in and keep us from our plans."

LET'S TALK ABOUT THIS

*What this story teaches:* We need friends, although sometimes they disappoint us for a while.

1. Why is it important for us to have friends? Why do we especially need them when we are in trouble or when we feel sad?

2. What did Maxi learn about friends? What did you learn about being a friend to others?

# For You and Me

MATTHEW 27:35-44, 55-56

"Nail Him to the cross!" the soldiers ordered.

"Crucify Him!" the Pharisees and their friends demanded.

"Spare Him!" Jesus' friends pleaded.

But Jesus was silent. Even when the Roman soldiers nailed His hands and feet to the cross.

"Father, forgive them, for they know not what they are doing," Jesus prayed for those who tormented Him.

The Roman soldiers looked ashamed when they heard that. "We kill Him and He prays for us to be forgiven?" they asked. "The others cursed us when we nailed them to the cross."

The soldiers picked up a sign that had been given to them. It read, "Jesus of Nazareth, the King of the Jews." Then they nailed it to His cross.

"I wonder if He is a king," one of them murmured.

"He certainly dies like one," said another.

When the cross was set in place, people began to gather beneath it to watch Jesus die. The Roman soldiers sat down to gamble for Jesus' robe.

"Why doesn't He save Himself?" the Pharisees and their friends said, mocking Him. "If He is the Son of God, let Him come down from the cross by Himself. Then we will believe in Him."

"That's true," some of the soldiers said. "If He is the king of the Jews, why doesn't He save Himself?"

Then one of the two robbers who were nailed to crosses beside Jesus began to say the same. "If You are God's Son, save Yourself and us."

The other robber looked quietly at Jesus. He had been watching Him. He had perhaps heard of Jesus and believed that He was God's Son.

"Remember me when You come into Your Kingdom," he asked Jesus quietly.

"Today you will be with Me in Paradise," Jesus answered.

The sky grew darker over the hill where Jesus was dying. By noon it was like twilight. Some people hurried away, frightened.

By midafternoon, Jesus cried out with a loud voice. "It is finished!" He said. "Father, I give My spirit into Your hands." When He had said that, Jesus died.

At that very time the earth began to tremble. Dead people arose from their tombs, and rocks crumbled. The soldiers were so frightened that some of them fell to the ground. The centurion, the leader of the soldiers, stared at the form of Jesus on the cross.

"He was the Son of God," he said softly.

Jesus had offered His life once and for all. Never again did another offering for sin need to be made.

The darkness gave way to a new light. At last men had a way to heaven, the only way, through Him.

WHAT DO YOU THINK?

*What this story teaches:* Jesus died as an offering for our sin, that we might have a way to heaven through Him.

1. Why did the centurion say that Jesus was God's Son? Why do you think the people beneath the cross should have believed in Him?

2. In what special way is Jesus' death important to all people? Who can get to heaven through Him?

# Ruff the Hero

Maxi sat up in bed and looked around. He was sure that he had heard some strange noise downstairs. But as much as he tried, Maxi could not hear it again.

*What should I do?* Maxi wondered. *Should I go downstairs to see what it is? Or should I wake Poppi?*

Maxi decided that he didn't want to wake Poppi just to tell him he thought he heard a noise. That seemed so foolish. No, he was sure that it would be better to go down and check things himself.

Quietly, Maxi slipped from bed and tiptoed down the carpeted stairway, with Ruff behind him. Maxi went so quietly that he could hardly hear himself breathe. But as soon as he went into the living room, Maxi said "oh" softly before he could catch himself. There, on the other side of the room, was the dark, shadowy form of a burglar.

The burglar swung around as soon as he heard Maxi. When he saw that Maxi was only a boy, he ran

for him. "I'll get you, you snoopy kid!" he growled. "I'll knock your brains out!" (Mini asked later how he could knock out something that wasn't there.)

But the burglar had not seen Ruff trot into the room behind Maxi. And Ruff had not seen the burglar until he saw him charging at Maxi. Suddenly Ruff exploded like a stick of dynamite (or "dog-a-mite," as Maxi called it), leaping on the burglar with an assortment of growls, barks, bites, and just plain noise.

Of course the noise brought Poppi into the room immediately. By this time the burglar decided that he had better find another home to rob. He flung poor Ruff against the wall as hard as he could, ran out the door, and got into a waiting car.

Now Mommi and Mini ran in, just in time to see Maxi bend over poor Ruff, who was lying still on the floor.

"Did someone kill our Ruff?" Mini asked.

Maxi put his ear against Ruff's chest to listen for his heartbeat. "He's alive. I can hear his heart beating," said Maxi.

Mommi brought some ice wrapped in a cloth to put on the bump on Ruff's head. Then all the Muffin Family gathered around Ruff to watch over and pray for him.

"Ruff could have been killed," Maxi said softly.

"And so could you," said Poppi. "I saw what happened. He was willing to die to protect you."

Maxi looked down at Ruff. "Oh, Ruff, to think you would die for me," he whispered. "I love you for doing that. Please get well."

"Is Ruff something like Jesus?" Mini whispered. "He did die for us."

"Something like Him," said Poppi. "But Jesus' death on the cross was not a sudden accident. God had planned that for a long time as a way of paying for our sins."

"But Jesus loved us enough to die for us, just like Ruff," Mini argued.

"Yes, in that way their willingness to die was the same," said Poppi. "And we love Jesus for doing that, just as Maxi loves Ruff for risking his life to save him."

Just then Ruff began to move. Before long, he stood on his feet and wobbled over to Maxi. Maxi threw his arms around Ruff and gave him a big hug.

"You'll always be a special friend," Maxi whispered to Ruff. "And Jesus will always be more special than ever because you helped me understand more what He did for me."

LET'S TALK ABOUT THIS

*What this story teaches:* We should love Jesus and accept the new life He gives, for He died to pay for our sins.

1. How did Ruff's brave act remind Mini and Maxi of Jesus' death?
2. How were the two actions different?
3. When you understand why Jesus died for you, what should you do about it? Will you?

# Who Will Roll the Stone Away?

JOHN 20:2-18

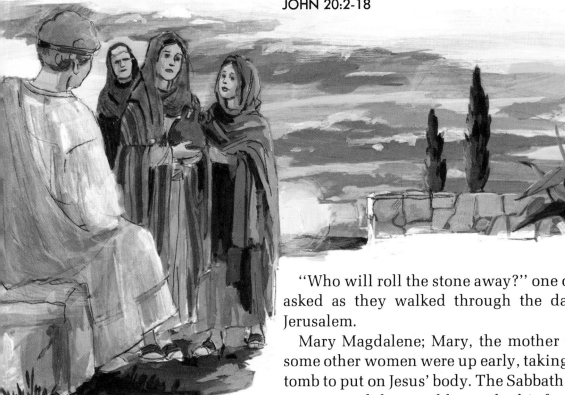

"Who will roll the stone away?" one of the women asked as they walked through the dark streets of Jerusalem.

Mary Magdalene; Mary, the mother of Jesus; and some other women were up early, taking spices to the tomb to put on Jesus' body. The Sabbath would end at sunrise, and they could now do this for the One they loved.

The great stone that was rolled over the entrance to the tomb could be a problem. They needed someone strong to roll it away.

Dawn was breaking as the women walked into the garden where the tomb was located. In the early morning light they could see the tomb ahead. Suddenly one of the women gave a cry.

"The stone!" she said. "It is rolled away."

The women ran toward the tomb as fast as they could go. Something was wrong. They must find out what had happened.

Suddenly they stopped. On a rock by the tomb sat a white-robed person whose face was as bright as lightning.

"An angel!" one of them said softly.

"You must not be afraid," the angel said. "You are looking for Jesus, but He is not here. He has risen from the dead, as He promised He would. Come with me, and I will show you the place where He lay."

The women followed quietly into the tomb. Jesus was certainly not there now. Instead, another angel sat by the place where Jesus had lain.

"You must not be so surprised," one angel told them. "Go tell Jesus' disciples and Peter that He has risen from the dead and is going to Galilee to meet you."

The women rushed from the tomb and almost ran back to the place where the disciples were meeting. "We saw two angels," they said. "And the tomb was empty, and Jesus has risen from the dead, and —"

The disciples shook their heads. What were these women saying? At last Peter and John spoke.

"Let's go to see this for ourselves," they said.

When they reached the tomb, they were amazed to see the cloth that had been wrapped around Jesus folded neatly, lying where He had left it. Puzzled, perhaps hopeful, they made their way back to the city, passing Mary Magdalene, who was returning alone to the tomb. Mary was sad, confused, and crying.

Suddenly Mary saw the two angels again. Now she was sure that this was really happening. She had not imagined all these things.

"Why are you crying?" the angels asked.

"Because someone has taken Jesus, and I don't know where they have gone with Him," she answered.

Behind her, Mary heard footsteps. She whirled around and saw a man standing in the path near the tomb.

"Why are you crying?" the man asked. "Are you looking for someone?"

"Please tell me where you have taken Him," Mary pleaded.

Then the man spoke her name. "Mary!" He said. It was the voice of Jesus. He was alive! Alive! Mary was so overcome with joy that she started to throw her arms around Him.

"I cannot stay long with you, for I must soon go back to heaven to live with My Father," Jesus told her. "Go tell your friends that I am alive again."

Mary raced through the garden and back to the city with the news that she had seen Jesus alive. There was no longer any question. He was alive again. And He would remain alive forever and ever.

WHAT DO YOU THINK?

*What this story teaches:* Jesus is alive and will never die again.

1. How do we know that Jesus is alive? How do we know that He will never die again?

2. Why is it important that Jesus arose from the dead? What if He had not risen? What difference would that make?

# Tulips

"Poppi."

"Yes, Mini."

"Doesn't this tulip smell good?"

"Buttery, Mini. You can tell it's a tulip by the way it smells."

"Poppi."

"What, Mini?"

"How can such a beautiful red flower come from dirt?"

"It doesn't. Tulips come from tulip bulbs. Mommi planted these last fall."

"But Poppi, those things she planted last fall weren't red. They were funny brown."

"I know, Mini. All colors of tulips come from those funny brown bulbs—yellow, white, red, pink, and even some with two colors."

"Poppi."

"Yes, Mini?"

"If Mommi planted red tulip bulbs, would they grow brown tulips?"

"No, Mini. God chose to make all His tulip bulbs about the same color. But He chose to make the tulips that come from them many colors."

"But Poppi, how can all those beautiful colors come from all those old, brown, dead things? And how do they know to do it in the spring?"

"God has some wonderful secrets, Mini. We don't know all of them. But we know that He does these things. So we can thank Him for doing them."

"Poppi."

"Yes, Mini."

"Remember the story you read last night?"

"About Jesus' coming back to life after He was dead?"

"That's the one, Poppi. And you know what? I was thinking about that story while we talked about tulips coming to life from those old, dead bulbs."

"Tulips can remind you of Jesus' resurrection every time you see them, Mini. But there is also a difference for you to remember."

"What's that, Poppi?"

"Your beautiful red tulip will soon die again. But Jesus is alive forever. He will never die again."

"Then Jesus is much more important than my red tulip, isn't He, Poppi?"

"Much more, Mini. Much, much more."

"Then I should love Him more, too, shouldn't I?"

"Yes, Mini. We all should. Then Jesus will give us a new life that never ends, too."

"I'm glad He gave me a new life when I asked Him, aren't you, Poppi?"

"Very glad, Mini. But now it's time to go inside and go to bed. Good night."

"Good night Poppi. Happy tulips!"

LET'S TALK ABOUT THIS

*What this story teaches:* Because Jesus is alive forever, He can give us a new life that will last forever.

1. How did the red tulip remind Mini of Jesus' new life?
2. How is the red tulip's new life different from Jesus' new life?
3. Have you asked Jesus for a new life that lasts forever? Why not now?

# Mini's Word List

Fourteen words that all Minis and Maxis want to know.

CANAANITES—People who lived in the Promised Land before the Israelites came from Egypt. They worshiped statues instead of God, sometimes in evil ways.

COMMUNION—A time of fellowship in our churches, when we remember the Lord's Supper.

CROSS—A large wooden pole with another pole tied across it. In Jesus' time, criminals were put to death by being nailed to a cross. This was called crucifixion. Jesus died on a cross, sent there by His enemies, who wanted Him to die like a criminal. But this was all part of God's plan to pay for our sins so we could be forgiven.

HOSANNA—When the Ark of the Covenant was brought to Jerusalem, and later when Jesus rode into Jerusalem, people shouted this greeting. It meant "Save us, we ask you."

LAMPSTAND—Sometimes called a candlestick. A stand on which ancient oil lamps were placed. These lamps were usually made of clay, with a wick at one end.

MESSIAH—Jesus is the Messiah, or Christ, who saves His people from their sins. *Messiah* is a Hebrew word that means the same thing as *Christ,* a Greek word.

PEACEMAKER—Someone who brings together two people who have been drawn apart by a quarrel or difference of opinion.

PRISON—A place where criminals are kept away from others. In Bible times, prisons were very dirty, and people often died there.

ROMANS—In Jesus' time, the people of Israel were ruled by the Romans, the people whose capital city was Rome. Rome is today in Italy.

SACRIFICE—Offering something to God. Hebrew people in Old Testament times killed and burned animals on an altar as a sacrifice.

SCRIPTURES—Another word for the Bible, God's Word. The word means "writing." In Jesus' time, the Scriptures were what we now call the Old Testament.

SINS—Wrong things that people do, which keep them away from God. These wrong things break God's rules.

STOREROOM—A room in which food or supplies are kept.

WILDERNESS—A desert or other wild place that has few trees and bushes. People usually do not live in a wilderness.